D̶I̶N̶O̶
FINDS

Consultant: Michael Brett-Surman
Illustrators: Robert Walters, Bruce J. Mohn, Stuart Armstrong

Copyright © 2000 by the National Geographic Society
Illustrations Copyright © 2000 by Robert F. Walters & Bruce J. Mohn

Published by
The National Geographic Society
John M. Fahey, Jr., President and Chief Executive Officer
Gilbert M. Grosvenor, Chairman of the Board
Nina D. Hoffman, Senior Vice President
William R. Gray, Vice President and Director, Book Division

Staff for this Book
Barbara Brownell, Director of Continuities
Marianne R. Koszorus, Senior Art Director
Toni Eugene, Editor
Alexandra Littlehales, Art Director
Patricia Fahy Frakes, Writer-Researcher
Susan V. Kelly, Illustrations Editor
Sharon Kocsis Berry, Illustrations Assistant
Mark A. Caraluzzi, Director of Direct Response Marketing
Heidi Vincent, Product Manager
Vincent P. Ryan, Manufacturing Manager
Lewis R. Bassford, Production Project Manager

Visit our Web site at www.nationalgeographic.com

Library of Congress Catalog Card Number: 00-133632
ISBN: 0-7922-3463-4

Color separations by Quad Graphics, Martinsburg, West Virginia
Printed in Mexico by R.R. Donnelley & Sons Company

MY FIRST POCKET GUIDE

DINO FINDS

PATRICIA FAHY FRAKES

Illustrations by Robert F. Walters and Bruce J. Mohn

NATIONAL GEOGRAPHIC SOCIETY

INTRODUCTION

You have seen pictures of dinosaurs in movies, in books, and on television. But no one has ever seen a live dinosaur. They lived millions of years ago. We know what dinosaurs looked like because of the detective work of scientists called paleontologists (pay-lee-on-TOL-o-jists). Each dinosaur discovery adds to our knowledge. Until *Giganotosaurus* was discovered, the largest known meat-eating dinosaur was *Tyrannosaurus*. Scientists once thought all dinosaurs had scaly skin, then they found some remains with feathers. Now they know that birds are the direct descendants of dinosaurs. Like a puzzle with a growing number of pieces, our knowledge of dinosaurs and their history grows more complete every day.

You may know about a lot of dinosaurs already, but this book tells you about some of the latest finds and reveals new information about earlier finds. You will also discover some animals that lived at the same time as dinosaurs.

HOW TO USE THIS BOOK

The animals in this book are arranged in the order that they lived on Earth—from the earliest to the most recent. Dinosaurs appear first, followed by some of the creatures that shared the world with them.

Each spread in the book tells you about one kind of animal. You will find out when it lived, its behavior, how to pronounce its name, what the name means, the size of the creature including its tail, and what it ate. A shaded map entry tells where and when its bones were first found. Silhouettes show the size of the animal compared to a man. The "Field Notes" entry adds a fact about the animal or find. If you do not know what a word means, you can look it up in the Glossary on page 76.

Tyrannosaurus

WHAT IS A FOSSIL?

Fossils are the preserved remains of ancient plants and animals. They provide the clues that scientists use to re-create the past. Fossils are often found in rock formations. A fossil forms when a plant or animal becomes covered with sand, mud, or other material soon after it dies. Slowly it turns to stone, and after many thousands of years, rain, rivers, and ice wear away some of the layers that cover it. Some fossils are found lying on the ground.

Fossil of
Oviraptor
on nest

To find others, scientists dig below the surface. Most fossils are the bones and shells of ancient animals. They are also the preserved outlines of plants and even footprints. Fossils show the vegetation that provided food for plant-eating dinosaurs. Animal fossils reveal not only what the creatures ate but also what may have wanted to eat them. Fossils of a dinosaur's teeth can help determine whether it ate meat or plants. Finding the bones of many of the same kind of dinosaur together indicates that they probably lived in groups. Recent finds of eggs even reveal how dinosaurs cared for their young.

Oviraptor

THE AGE OF DINOSAURS

Fossils dating from the time before there were dinosaurs can give us a picture of what the Earth was like then. There were many vertebrates—animals with backbones—but none like the giants to come. As some kinds of animals died off, others replaced them. The first dinosaurs appeared about 225 million years ago, and the last died out about 65 million years ago. That means dinosaurs were around for 160 million years. This time is called the Age of Dinosaurs. Its scientific name is the Mesozoic (MEZ-uh-ZOH-ik) era. It is divided into three parts: The Triassic (tri-ASS-ik), the Jurassic (jur-ASS-ik), and the Cretaceous (cree-TAY-shus) periods.

TIME LINE OF LIFE ON EARTH

MILLIONS OF YEARS AGO	ERA	PERIOD	
Present			
1.64	Cenozoic	Quaternary	Humans appear
	Cenozoic	Tertiary	Age of mammals
65			
145	Mesozoic	Cretaceous	Dinosaurs die out
208	Mesozoic	Jurassic	Dinosaurs dominate
245	Mesozoic	Triassic	Dinosaurs appear
290	Palaeozoic	Permian	Mammal-like reptiles dominate
362	Palaeozoic	Carboniferous	Reptiles appear
408	Palaeozoic	Devonian	Fishes dominate
439	Palaeozoic	Silurian	Giant sea scorpions; first plants
510	Palaeozoic	Ordovician	First animals with backbones
570	Palaeozoic	Cambrian	First animals with shells
610	Proterozoic	Vendian	First soft-bodied animals
2500	Proterozoic	1000	First animal traces
4000	Archaean	3500	First algae and bacteria
4600			Origin of the earth

At the beginning of the Mesozoic era, one huge landmass called Pangaea (pan-JEE-uh) existed on Earth. As millions of years passed, this landmass broke up into the seven continents we know today. This is why the same kinds of dinosaurs are sometimes found on different continents.

Dinosaurs first appeared during the Triassic period. These were lively little two legged meat-eating animals. Then came the Jurassic, when large plant-eaters walked on all fours and roamed in groups. The climate grew wetter, and shallow seas spread over the land.

During the Cretaceous, small and large meat-eaters, long-necked and two-footed plant-eaters, and dinosaurs with armor and horns roamed the Earth. Then, the dinosaurs and many other kinds of plants and animals, vanished. Scientists still do not know why. Maybe the climate changed. Perhaps a meteorite hit the Earth. Perhaps volcanic eruptions killed off life.

Every new dino find provides more clues to why and how the Age of Dinosaurs ended.

MELANOROSAURUS

 Largest known dinosaur of the Triassic period, *Melanorosaurus* ate plants. It walked on all fours, but its front legs were short, so that it ran on its two longer hind legs.

FIELD NOTES

Like all dinosaurs this one lived on land and had legs that extended straight down from its body.

Melanorosaurus lived in forests. It stretched its neck to munch near the tops of trees.

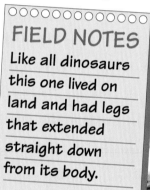

AFRICA

Melanorosaurus fossils were found in Africa and named in 1924. Recent ones were found in 1993.

WHAT TO LOOK FOR:

✴ NAME
Melanorosaurus (me-LAN-or-o-SORE-us) means "black mountain lizard." The dinosaur was named after the place where it was found.

✴ SIZE
Melanorosaurus was 40 feet long.

✴ DIET
Melanorosaurus was a plant-eater.

✴ MORE
Scientists have not yet unearthed a skull of this dinosaur.

SYNTARSUS

 Long-legged *Syntarsus* was a medium-size, lightly built, dinosaur. It lived and hunted with others of its kind in the desert. A group of these dinosaurs was made up of both males and females.

Fossil finds show that these dinosaurs may have hunted in groups so that they could kill larger animals.

WHERE AND WHEN:
Schoolboys in Africa found the first *Syntarsus* bones in 1963. More were unearthed in Arizona in 1977.

WHAT TO LOOK FOR:

✳ NAME
Syntarsus (sin-TAR-sus) means "fused" or "flat" ankle. These dinosaurs had ankles similar to those of modern birds and ran like they run today.

✳ SIZE
Syntarsus was about 10 feet long and weighed 60 to 70 pounds.

✳ DIET
Syntarsus was a meat-eating hunter.

✳ MORE
Syntarsus was a fast runner.

FIELD NOTES

It used its strong front legs, or arms, and sharp claws to attack and hang on to its prey.

XIAOSAURUS

 Little *Xiaosaurus* had feet like a bird, a beak like a bird, and walked on two long legs. The front legs of dinosaurs varied in length. Those of *Xiaosaurus* were short.

ASIA

WHERE AND WHEN:
Xiaosaurus fossils were found in China in 1980. In 1991 scientists confirmed it was a new type of dinosaur.

WHAT TO LOOK FOR:

✻ NAME
Xiaosaurus (she-ow-SORE-us) means "little" or "early" lizard.

✻ SIZE
Xiaosaurus was about 3½ feet long, including its tail.

✻ DIET
Xiaosaurus ate ferns and other plants.

✻ MORE
The tail of *Xiaosaurus* made up half the length of its body and helped it to balance as it ran.

To protect itself from predators, *Xiaosaurus* hid beneath the branches and leaves of ferns and bushes.

TUOJIANGOSAURUS

Tuojiangosaurus was the size of a small truck. It had a short neck and dined on plants that grew close to the ground. A double row of cone-shaped plates protected it from enemies that tried to sneak up on it.

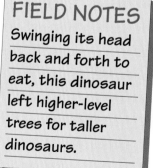

FIELD NOTES

Swinging its head back and forth to eat, this dinosaur left higher-level trees for taller dinosaurs.

Tuojiangosaurus could have used its long spiked tail as a weapon to fight off the ferocious meat-eating dinosaurs that were its enemies.

WHERE AND WHEN:

Tuojiangosaurus was found in central China in 1977. Since then, many dinosaurs have been found there.

WHAT TO LOOK FOR:

✳ NAME

Tuojiangosaurus (Twoh-jyang-o-SAWR-us) is named after the river where it was found.

✳ SIZE

Tuojiangosaurus was 24 feet long and 7 feet tall.

✳ DIET

Tuojiangosaurus had small, weak teeth and ate only soft plants.

✳ MORE

Tuojiangosaurus walked on four feet.

CAMPTOSAURUS

Imagine a car-size dinosaur with a horse-like head and a bird-like beak. *Camptosaurus* was the first of many large, two-legged plant-eaters with thick, powerful legs.

Camptosaurus ate vegetation, both high and low, biting it off with its beak then slicing it up with dozens of sharp teeth.

WHERE AND WHEN:
A *Camptosaurus* was found in Wyoming in 1879. More have been found in western America and Europe.

WHAT TO LOOK FOR:

✳ NAME
Camptosaurus (kamp-tow-SAWR-us) means "flexible lizard."

✳ SIZE
Camptosaurus was 23 feet long and may have weighed as much as a thousand pounds.

✳ DIET
Camptosaurus was a plant-eater.

✳ MORE
It ran on two legs and sometimes got down on all fours to reach low plants.

FIELD NOTES
Over time, some dinosaurs developed hoofs. Camptosaurus's hand had begun that change.

GARGOYLEOSAURUS

 *Gargoyleosaurus* had a covering of cone-shaped plates on its body and armor over its eyes, head, and jaw. An enemy would have broken its teeth on this dinosaur.

WHERE AND WHEN:
Gargoyleosaurus was found in Wyoming in 1997. It was a relative of the better known *Ankylosaurus*.

WHAT TO LOOK FOR:

✳ **NAME**
Gargoyleosaurus (gahr-GOI-lee-oh-SAWR-us) was named after carvings of monsters, called gargoyles, that often decorate the outer walls of churches.

✳ **SIZE**
Gargoyleosaurus was ten feet long.

✳ **DIET**
A plant-eater, it used its narrow beak to snap off the most tender parts to eat.

✳ **MORE**
It had a tiny, triangular-shaped head.

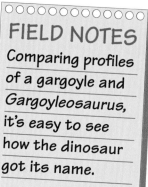

FIELD NOTES

Comparing profiles of a gargoyle and Gargoyleosaurus, it's easy to see how the dinosaur got its name.

Thick spines sticking out from its sides could protect this dinosaur when enemies attacked.

OTHNIELIA

 Othnielia was so small it could fit in your lap. Its main defense was to hide from its enemies. This little dinosaur used its long, stiff tail for balance when it was running.

These dinosaurs lived in groups. They may have confused their enemies by running off in different directions.

FIELD NOTES

The head of *Othnielia* was smaller than a man's hand. The dinosaur's tiny jaw held 56 teeth!

WHERE AND WHEN:

NORTH AMERICA

This fossil was discovered in Colorado in 1877. More fossils were found in the West in 1977.

WHAT TO LOOK FOR:

✳ NAME
Othnielia (OTH-nee-LEE-uh) was named for Othniel Charles Marsh, a famous paleontologist.

✳ SIZE
Othnielia was three feet in length, including its long tail.

✳ DIET
Othnielia was a plant-eater.

✳ MORE
Claws on its hands and feet helped it grip plants and defend itself.

TORVOSAURUS

 Size, powerful arms, and three claws on each hand helped this dinosaur attack the plant-eaters it ate. *Torvosaurus* had short arms—about the length of a man's.

WHERE AND WHEN:
Scientists discovered the first *Torvosaurus* fossil in Colorado in 1979. In 1985 they found more fossils.

NORTH AMERICA

WHAT TO LOOK FOR:

✳ **NAME**
Torvosaurus (tor-vo-SORE-us) means "savage lizard."

✳ **SIZE**
Torvosaurus was about as long as an *Allosaurus*—30 feet—but heavier.

✳ **DIET**
Torvosaurus was a meat-eater.

✳ **MORE**
In addition to killing other animals for food, *Torvosaurus* was a scavenger—it ate animals that were already dead.

Three short, thick fingers on each of its hands were equipped with 12-inch claws.

JOBARIA

Jobaria reared up like a modern elephant to reach the tops of the tallest trees. It may also have reared up and used its heavy, powerful front legs to crash down on smaller predators.

FIELD NOTES

Jobaria could have wounded meat-eating enemies with the sharp claws on each of its front feet.

Now a dry hot desert, the forests and rivers of the past were a rich home for *Jobaria*.

26

WHERE AND WHEN:
In 1997 some 20 tons of
Jobaria fossils were found
in Nigeria and shipped to
the United States for study.

AFRICA

WHAT TO LOOK FOR:

✳ NAME
Jobaria (jo-BAR-ee-a) is named for
Jobar, a legendary creature of the
Tuareg nomads who live in Nigeria.

✳ SIZE
Jobaria was 60 to 70 feet long and
weighed 40,000 pounds.

✳ DIET
Jobaria was such a huge plant-eater that
it probably had to eat all day long.

✳ MORE
Jobaria was as long as a tennis court.

SAUROPOSEIDON

Sauroposeidon had such a long neck and was so huge that it could have peeked in the top-floor window of a six-story building. This dinosaur was four times as big as a modern giraffe.

Sauroposeidon dined on the tallest trees and towering tree ferns. It ate a ton of plants every day.

WHERE AND WHEN:
The first *Sauroposeidon* fossil was found by an employee of a state prison in Oklahoma in 1994.

NORTH
AMERICA

WHAT TO LOOK FOR:

✴ NAME
Sauroposeidon (SORE-o-po-SIGH-dun) means "lizard earthquake god."

✴ SIZE
This giant was 60 feet tall and weighed 60 tons.

✴ DIET
Sauroposeidon ate evergreens and leaves from flowering trees.

✴ MORE
Sauroposeidon only had to stretch its long neck to reach even the tallest trees.

FIELD NOTES

The neck bones were up to four feet long. They were filled with air pockets, which made them light.

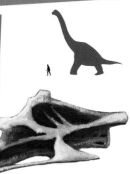

SUCHOMIMUS

 Suchomimus lived next to a huge inland sea in Africa. It had a head like a crocodile but a body like a dinosaur. It ran on two legs on land but waded into the water on all fours to catch fish to eat.

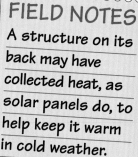

```
○○○○○○○○○○○○○
FIELD NOTES
A structure on its
back may have
collected heat, as
solar panels do, to
help keep it warm
in cold weather.
```

Like bears catching salmon today, *Suchomimus* hooked fish with its huge claws.

AFRICA

WHAT TO LOOK FOR:

✱ NAME
Suchomimus (sook-oh-MIME-us) means "crocodile imitator."

✱ SIZE
Suchomimus was 36 feet long. Its head was 4 feet long.

✱ DIET
Suchomimus ate mostly fish and other reptiles.

✱ MORE
Suchomimus probably competed with crocodiles for food.

SINORNITHOSAURUS

Most dinosaurs had scaly skin, but *Sinornithosaurus* had a downy coat. Dinosaurs like this one were so bird-like that scientists decided birds developed from them.

WHERE AND WHEN:

ASIA

Sinornithosaurus was found embedded in a rock formation in northeastern China in 1999.

WHAT TO LOOK FOR:

✴ **NAME**
Sinornithosaurus (sine-or-NITH-o-SORE-us) means "China bird lizard."

✴ **SIZE**
Sinornithosaurus was five feet long—about the size of an eagle.

✴ **DIET**
Sinornithosaurus, like eagles and hawks today, was a meat-eater.

✴ **MORE**
Dagger-like teeth and long, curved claws made *Sinornithosaurus* a fierce predator.

Sinornithosaurus could move its front legs up and down much as a bird flaps its wings.

SINOSAUROPTERYX

 This chicken-size dinosaur had a feathery fringe running from the top of its skull to its long tail. These early feathers did not help it fly, but they may have helped it blend in with the plants around it.

FIELD NOTES

Its unusual hair-like feathers could have helped keep Sinosauropteryx warm when it was cold outside.

From remains found in its stomach, scientists know this dinosaur dined on lizards and small mammals.

WHERE AND WHEN:
Sinosauropteryx was found in China in 1996. After studying it for two years, scientists named it in 1998.

WHAT TO LOOK FOR:

✳ NAME
Sinosauropteryx (sign-o-sore-OP-ter-ix) means "China lizard wing."

✳ SIZE
It was four feet long, including its tail.

✳ DIET
Sinosauropteryx was a meat-eater. The fossil contained remains of a lizard and a small mammal it had eaten.

✳ MORE
Scientists found eggs inside a female *Sinosauropteryx*.

PROTARCHAEOPTERYX

Scientists at first thought *Protarchaeopteryx* was an early flightless bird. Studies proved that it was one of many bird-like dinosaurs.

WHERE AND WHEN:

ASIA

Protarchaeopteryx was found in the bottom of an ancient lake bed in northeastern China in 1997.

WHAT TO LOOK FOR:

✱ NAME
Its name (prote-ark-ee-OP-ter-ix) means "first archaeopteryx." *Archaeopteryx* was the earliest known bird.

✱ SIZE
Protarchaeopteryx was the size of a small chicken.

✱ DIET
Protarchaeopteryx was a meat-eater.

✱ MORE
Its feathers were all the same length, like those of flightless birds today.

Its feathers, hollow bones, and beak provide more evidence that birds developed directly from the dinosaurs.

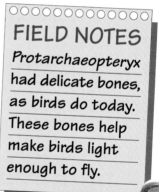

FIELD NOTES

Protarchaeopteryx had delicate bones, as birds do today. These bones help make birds light enough to fly.

GIGANOTOSAURUS

 The biggest meat-eating dinosaur ever found, *Giganotosaurus* stood 12 feet tall at the hips and weighed 16,000 pounds. Its arms were so short it would have had a hard time pushing itself up if it fell. down.

WHERE AND WHEN:

SOUTH AMERICA

A local auto mechanic found the fossil remains of *Giganotosaurus* in southern Argentina in 1995.

WHAT TO LOOK FOR:

＊ NAME
Giganotosaurus (jig-a-NO-toe-SORE-us) means "giant south lizard."

＊ SIZE
Giganotosaurus was 47 feet long—7 feet bigger than *Tyrannosaurus rex*.

＊ DIET
This giant meat-eater probably dined on large and small plant-eaters.

＊ MORE
Giganotosaurus had a tiny brain. It was about the size and shape of a banana.

Giganotosaurus moved about on two legs and had huge jaws lined with jagged teeth eight inches long.

CAUDIPTERYX

 Caudipteryx had feathers covering its very short arms, most of its body, and its short tail. Like all bird-like dinosaurs, it walked and ran on its two back legs.

WHERE AND WHEN:
Caudipteryx was found in northeastern China in 1998 with a number of other kinds of bird-like dinosaurs.

ASIA

WHERE AND WHEN:

✳ **NAME**
Caudipteryx (caw-DIP-ter-ix) means, "tail feather."

✳ **SIZE**
Caudipteryx was about three feet long.

✳ **DIET**
Caudipteryx was a meat-eater. Like birds today it had pebbles in its stomach that helped it grind up food.

✳ **MORE**
It may offer clues to how dinosaurs might have developed into birds.

Caudipteryx was light, and it ran very fast. Its "wings" were much too small to lift it off the ground.

ALTIRHINUS

A middle-size plant-eater, *Altirhinus* looked very different because of its big, high-arched nose. Its nose was so huge that scientists have concluded this dinosaur had a very good sense of smell.

FIELD NOTES

Spikes three inches long on the thumbs of this dinosaur helped it slash out at enemies.

Altirhinus ate and lived in a group made up of males and females.

ASIA

Altirhinus was discovered in Kazakhstan in the 1950s. More fossils were found there in the 1990s.

WHAT TO LOOK FOR:

✳ NAME
Altirhinus (al-ti-RINE-us) means "high snout."

✳ SIZE
Altirhinus was about 23 to 26 feet long—twice as long as a Volkswagen.

✳ DIET
Altirhinus browsed on low plants.

✳ MORE
Altirhinus had a curved little finger it could wind around food to grasp it and and hold on tight.

CARNOTAURUS

Carnotaurus charged through its world like a huge bull. It was covered with rows of studs that stuck up from the sides of its neck, back, and tail.

WHERE AND WHEN:
The first *Carnotaurus* fossil was found in Argentina in 1984. Only the feet were were missing.

SOUTH AMERICA

WHAT TO LOOK FOR:

✳ **NAME**
Carnotaurus (car-no-TORE-us) means, "flesh bull."

✳ **SIZE**
Carnotaurus was 20 to 40 feet long.

✳ **DIET**
Carnotaurus was a meat-eater.

✳ **MORE**
Unlike most large dinosaurs, *Carnotaurus* had very thick and very short arms. They were only about ten inches long.

Carnotaurus males may have butted each other with their sharp horns to determine which one was stronger.

FIELD NOTES

From skin impressions in the rock, scientists could tell that its armor was rows of large scales.

ANATOTITAN

Anatotitan weighed 16,000 pounds. It was a type of dinosaur with a duck-shaped bill. It usually walked on two legs, but got down on all fours when it was eating.

Anatotitan used its shovel-shaped mouth to scoop up all the plants it needed to stay alive.

Ranchers in South Dakota discovered it in 1882. They told scientists where it was in exchange for a pistol.

WHAT TO LOOK FOR:

✳ NAME
Anatotitan (a-NAT-o-TIE-tan) means "duck" and "titan," the name for a mythical Greek giant.

✳ SIZE
Anatotitan was 40 feet long and weighed more than an elephant.

✳ DIET
Anatotitan ate pine needles and twigs.

✳ MORE
When it was found, its ribs were sticking up out of the ground like a picket fence.

FIELD NOTES

Anatotitan had hundreds of teeth in its cheeks to grind up the tough plants that made up its diet.

ACHELOUSAURUS

 This rhinoceros-like creature moved very slowly on four legs like huge tree trunks. *Achelousaurus* had a frill, a big bump on its nose, and a beak like a parrot.

WHERE AND WHEN:
Achelousaurus fossils were first found in Montana in 1995. More have been found in the western U.S.

NORTH AMERICA

WHAT TO LOOK FOR:

❋ NAME
Achelousaurus (ah-key-loh-SAWR-us) was named for a Greek god who lost a horn in a fight with Hercules.

❋ SIZE
Achelousaurus was about 20 feet long.

❋ DIET
Achelousaurus was a plant-eater.

❋ MORE
A large round knob of bone on its snout was all that was left of the much larger horns found in earlier dinosaurs.

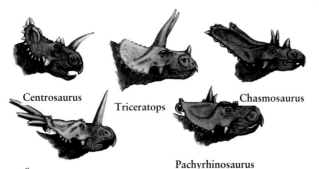

Centrosaurus

Triceratops

Chasmosaurus

Styracosaurus

Pachyrhinosaurus

Two long spikes that faced backward protected the neck of this dinosaur.

49

BAGACERATOPS

 Bagaceratops was a small dinosaur with a heavy body and a long tail. It displayed miniature versions of the nose horns, head shields, and frills found on much larger dinosaurs.

WHERE AND WHEN:

Scientists discovered 22 skulls and other bones, most of them from young animals, in Mongolia in 1975.

WHAT TO LOOK FOR:

✳ **NAME**
Bagaceratops (bah-gah-SEHR-uh-tops) means "small horned face."

✳ **SIZE**
Bagaceratops was about two feet long.

✳ **DIET**
Bagaceratops was a plant-eater.

✳ **MORE**
Though it was the size of a large cat, *Bagaceratops* looked very different, with a small horn on its snout, no teeth at the front of its mouth, and a tough beak.

Bagaceratops was so small a man could easily trip over it. It had a head shaped like a triangle.

Bagaceratops hatched from a five-inch-long egg. Like a bird today, it had to break out of its shell.

INGENIA

Ingenia had light, hollow bones and a bird-like, beaked skull. Muscular back legs enabled it to run fast, and curving fingers and claws on its large front hands helped it hold onto its prey.

FIELD NOTES

Like most birds today, *Ingenia* laid eggs and sat on its nest to protect them until they hatched.

Ingenia is one of a series of bird-like dinosaurs that have been discovered in Mongolia and China in recent years.

ASIA

WHAT TO LOOK FOR:

✳ NAME
Ingenia (in-GAY-nee-a) was named for a region in Mongolia.

✳ SIZE
Ingenia was about 3½ feet tall.

✳ DIET
It was a meat-eater. Early reports said it also stole and ate eggs.

✳ MORE
The spaces in *Ingenia*'s skull were huge. They show that the baby dinosaur's eyes took up half the space in its head.

PRENOCEPHALE

 The hard dome of this dinosaur's skull, covered with small knobs, was a great weapon when males had head-butting contests to decide which was stronger.

WHERE AND WHEN:
Female paleontologists found the first *Prenocephale* in Mongolia in 1969. More bones were found in 1990.

ASIA

WHAT TO LOOK FOR:

✳ NAME
Prenocephale (preen-o-SEF-uh-lee) means "sloping head."

✳ SIZE
Prenocephale was about eight feet long.

✳ DIET
Its diet included fruits, leaves, and insects.

✳ MORE
Like most plant-eaters, *Prenocephale* had eyes that faced sideways so that it could keep a lookout for predators.

Heads lowered, males may have fought to determine the leader of the group.

FIELD NOTES

When scientists found the fossil skull of this dinosaur, it looked like a stone that had been polished.

QUAESITOSAURUS

Quaesitosaurus was a land dweller. Only the skull of this dinosaur has been discovered. Until scientists find more bones of *Quaesitosaurus,* they can only guess at how it looked.

Quaesitosaurus had a nose far from its mouth—high on its head near its eyes—so that it could eat and breathe at the same time.

WHERE AND WHEN:
It was found in the Gobi, a desert in Mongolia, in 1983. No other *Quaesitosaurus* fossils have been discovered.

WHAT TO LOOK FOR:

✳ NAME
Quaesitosaurus (kwee-sit-o-SAWR-us) means "uncommon lizard."

✳ SIZE
Its exact size is not known because only its skull was found.

✳ DIET
Quaesitosaurus ate soft plants.

✳ MORE
Scientists rarely find fossil skulls because they are more delicate and don't last as long as fossils of other parts of the body.

FIELD NOTES

A large ear opening directly below this dinosaur's eye could mean that the animal had excellent hearing.

THERIZINOSAURUS

 *Therizinosaurus* had curved claws on its hands. Each claw was about the size of a baseball bat. The claws were shaped like a scythe—a tool used to cut long grass.

WHERE AND WHEN:

ASIA

A fossil arm was found in Mongolia in 1954. Other parts of the animal have since been found there.

WHAT TO LOOK FOR:

✴ NAME
Therizinosaurus (ther-i-ZIN-o-SAWR-us) means "scythe lizard."

✴ SIZE
Therizinosaurus is thought to have been about 20 feet long.

✴ DIET
Therizinosaurus was a meat-eater. It may also have eaten plants and insects.

✴ MORE
Scientists first thought its claws were those of a giant turtle.

The 27-inch claws of *Therizinosaurus* could slash apart its enemies—the many other meat-eating dinosaurs.

00000000000000

FIELD NOTES

Therizinosaurus may have used its sharp claws to tear up insect mounds looking for tasty snacks.

OTHER ANIMALS

When you see dinosaurs on television or in movies or books, it often looks as if they were the only kind of wild animals on Earth. On shows such as the *The Flintstones* and *Barney & Friends*, dinosaurs are surrounded by human beings. Both impressions are wrong.

The truth is that dinosaurs appeared and then disappeared millions of years before the first humans set foot on Earth. And many varieties of bugs, fish, turtles, crocodiles, and flying reptiles lived at the same time that dinosaurs ruled the Earth.

Most of these creatures had been around much longer than dinosaurs—and some survived long after dinosaurs all died out, or became extinct. Many more animals developed on Earth after dinosaurs died out.

Even the furry animals we know as mammals shared the world of the dinosaurs. But those mammals were small, and there were only a few different kinds. Mammals began to develop during the Cretaceous period, and it wasn't until dinosaurs disappeared from the Earth that large mammals began to replace the huge reptiles.

This section of the book introduces you to some of the animals that lived during the time of the dinosaurs. Many of them disappeared along with the dinosaurs. And some have relatives that are still living today.

LYSTROSAURUS

 Fossils of this small, pig-like reptile have been found on every continent except Europe. Finding fossils in such wide areas is evidence that these continents were once joined in one huge landmass.

WHERE AND WHEN:
Lystrosaurus fossils were found in North America in the 1870s. Later finds were made on other continents.

NORTH AMERICA

WHAT TO LOOK FOR:

✳ NAME
Lystrosaurus (LISS-tro-SORE-us) means "trowel lizard." This creature's beak was shaped like a shovel.

✳ SIZE
Lystrosaurus was about three feet long.

✳ DIET
Lystrosaurus was a plant-eater.

✳ MORE
It probably lived and browsed near lakes and swamps in a group with others of its kind.

Once, scientists thought that *Lystrosaurus* wallowed in the water to find its meals.

FIELD NOTES

Scientists now think this dinosaur used its two tusk-like teeth to burrow in the ground to find food.

GERROTHORAX

Gerrothorax looked like a large, flat tadpole. It hid in sand and mud on the bottom of streams waiting to catch fish in its gaping jaws.

WHERE AND WHEN:

EUROPE

The first *Gerrothorax* was found in Sweden in 1934. Fossils were later discovered in England and Germany.

WHAT TO LOOK FOR:

✳ NAME
Gerrothorax (jer-o-THOR-ax) means "shield-shaped body."

✳ SIZE
Gerrothorax was about three feet long.

✳ DIET
Gerrothorax was a meat-eater. It survived on fish.

✳ MORE
It could breathe underwater. Like fish, it had gills, organs that take oxygen from the water.

Gerrothorax could look straight up because its eyes were on the top of its flat head.

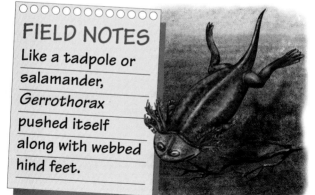

FIELD NOTES
Like a tadpole or salamander, *Gerrothorax* pushed itself along with webbed hind feet.

PROTOSUCHUS

This early crocodile had strong jaws and teeth like daggers that snapped down on the small creatures that were its main diet. Unlike modern crocodiles, *Protosuchus* lived only on land.

FIELD NOTES

Like crocodiles today, it had two teeth in its lower jaw that fit into notches in its upper jaw.

This creature, like dinosaurs, had straighter legs than those of modern crocodiles.

WHERE AND WHEN:
Scientists heard about *Protosuchus* from a Navajo Indian who found the first fossils in Arizona in 1934.

NORTH AMERICA

WHAT TO LOOK FOR:

✳ NAME
Protosuchus (pro-toh-SOOK-us) means "first crocodile."

✳ SIZE
Protosuchus was about three feet long.

✳ DIET
It was a meat-eater and probably ate small dinosaurs and other reptiles.

✳ MORE
Protosuchus had short legs and rows of bony plates that protected its back and belly.

STENOPTERYGIUS

Stenopterygius was a reptile that lived in the ocean. Its large eyes helped it spot dinner easily in the lighter areas near the surface, where the sun's rays could reach.

EUROPE

WHERE AND WHEN:
Stenopterygius fossils were found in1904 in a part of Germany that was a sea in ancient times.

WHAT TO LOOK FOR:

✳ NAME
Stenopterygius (sten-op-teh-RIDGE-ee-us) means "narrow paddle."

✳ SIZE
It was about ten feet long.

✳ DIET
It ate fish, squid-like creatures, and other fast-swimming animals.

✳ MORE
Stenopterygius did not lay eggs as dinosaurs did. It gave birth to live young in the water.

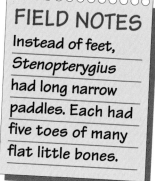

Though it swam
easily, this big
reptile could
not breathe
underwater and
had to come up to
the surface for a
gulp of fresh air.

FIELD NOTES
Instead of feet,
Stenopterygius
had long narrow
paddles. Each had
five toes of many
flat little bones.

KRONOSAURUS

 Kronosaurus had a huge head but was still a speedy swimmer. Its body was shaped like a torpedo, and its massive, paddle-shaped legs propelled it through the water.

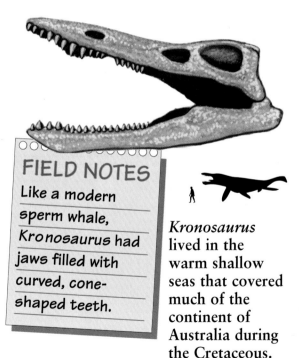

FIELD NOTES

Like a modern sperm whale, Kronosaurus had jaws filled with curved, cone-shaped teeth.

Kronosaurus lived in the warm shallow seas that covered much of the continent of Australia during the Cretaceous.

WHERE AND WHEN:
Kronosaurus was found in Australia in 1889 and 1927. More fossils were discovered in South America in 1992.

AUSTRALIA

WHAT TO LOOK FOR:

✷ **NAME**
Kronosaurus (krone-uh-SORE-us) was named for the mythical giant Kronos, who ate his own children.

✷ **SIZE**
Kronosaurus was 30 feet long.

✷ **DIET**
Kronosaurus was a meat-eater. It ate other sea creatures and its own kind.

✷ **MORE**
Rounded teeth at the back of its huge jaws were used to crush shells.

ARCHELON

 Archelon was the largest sea turtle ever discovered. It was as big as a car. Archelon had a shell of bony ribs covered by thick, rubbery skin.

WHERE AND WHEN:

NORTH AMERICA

Archelon was first found in South Dakota in 1896. In ancient times that area was covered by a huge ocean.

WHAT TO LOOK FOR:

✳ NAME
The name *Archelon* (AR-key-lon) means "ancient turtle."

✳ SIZE
Archelon was 12 feet long.

✳ DIET
It ate jellyfish and other slow-moving sea creatures.

✳ MORE
Archelon's paddle-shaped legs were way too big to pull inside its shell the way some modern turtles can.

Archelon stroked its big, heavy front flippers up and down like a penguin to move through the water.

73

QUETZALCOATLUS

Quetzalcoatlus was the largest flying vertebrate, or animal with a backbone, ever. It soared on enormously long wings. Like a modern vulture, it had good eyesight and could spot prey from great heights.

It weighed about 190 pounds, but it could soar like an eagle on its long, narrow wings.

WHERE AND WHEN:
Fossils of *Quetzalcoatlus* were found in Big Bend National Park, in southern Texas, in 1972.

NORTH AMERICA

WHAT TO LOOK FOR:

✳ NAME
*Quetzalcoatlu*s (ket-zall-co-AT-lus) was named for a Mexican god.

✳ SIZE
It measured 39 feet from the tip of one wing to the tip of the other.

✳ DIET
Quetzalcoatlus ate carrion—animals that were already dead.

✳ MORE
Its long, narrow head could reach far inside a dead animal to tear out meat.

FIELD NOTES

Quetzalcoatlus had three small fingers on each wing. Long fourth fingers supported its wings.

GLOSSARY

aquatic Growing, living in, or spending time in fresh water.

armor A protective outer layer.

browse To search for plants at or near head height.

carrion Dead and rotting animals.

crest A ridge that sticks out of a skull or tooth.

flexible Capable of bending.

flesh The soft parts of the body, between the skin and the bones.

fossil The preserved remains of an animal or plant that lived long ago.

mammal An animal, usually with hair or fur, that feeds its young on milk from the mother's body.

plates Thin, flat pieces of bone.

predator An animal that hunts and kills other animals for food.

prey An animal that is hunted by other animals for food.

reptile An animal that has scaly or leathery skin and usually lays eggs. Snakes and lizards are reptiles.

scavenge To eat dead animals left by other predators.

swamp An area of wetland with many trees and shrubs.

vegetation All the plants that grow in an area.

vertebrate An animal—fish, amphibian, reptile, bird, or mammal—with a backbone, or spinal column.

INDEX OF
DINO FINDS

ABOUT THE CONSULTANT

Dr. Michael Brett-Surman, a professor at George Washington University in Washington, D.C., is a dinosaur paleontologist. He has named three dinosaurs—*Secernosaurus, Gilmoreosaurus,* and *Anatotitan*—and is the coeditor of two award-winning books, *The Complete Dinosaur* and *James Gurney—The World of Dinosaurs.*
As a consultant, Dr. Brett-Surman has worked with publishers in the United States, Canada, the United Kingdom, and Japan. He has appeared more than 50 times in magazines and newspapers and on radio, television, and video. His popular lecture "Dinosaurs for Parents, Teachers and other Living Fossils" has been presented in many states.

ILLUSTRATIONS CREDITS